Heal Endometriosis Naturally

Cookbook

With Over 101 Wheat,
Gluten & Soy FREE Recipes

Wendy K Laidlaw

1 Cup - ~~8¾ oz~~ 340g 12oz

3/4 " 255g 90z

2/3" 227g 80z

1/2 " 170g 60z

©Copyright 2016 Wendy K Laidlaw

All Rights Reserved.

ISBN-13: 978-1530979219
ISBN-10: 1530979218

No part of this publication may be reproduced, distributed, or transmitted in any for or by any means, including photocopying, recording or other electronic or mechanical methods, without the express prior written permission of the author, except in the case of brief quotations embodied in critical reviews and certain other noncommercial uses permitted by copyright law.

Other Books by Wendy K Laidlaw
Heal Endometriosis Naturally Without Painkillers, Drugs or Surgery (2015)
ISBN - 10: 1515385698   ISBN - 13: 978-1515385691

Edited by Maxine I K Anderson

For all permissions and requests, please write to the author at;-
Wendy@HealEndometriosisNaturally.com
www.HealEndometriosisNaturally.com

MEDICAL DISCLAIMER

THIS BOOK IS BASED ON MY PERSONAL EXPERIENCES ONLY,
AND SHOULD NOT BE USED TO TAKE THE PLACE OF A PROFESSIONAL'S
OPINION.

The information should not be treated as professional medical advice – it is only my experience and the recommended recipes for healthy eating are to be used in conjunction with a healthy lifestyle, supplementation of appropriate vitamins and minerals, and the removal of all known toxins.

- This book is not intended as a substitute for the medical advice of physicians or doctors, although I would suggest you also seek a medical professional who is supportive of your desire to consider a natural approach to healing and changing their food habits and diet. The reader should regularly consult a physician or doctor in matters relating to her health and particularly, with respect to any symptoms that may require diagnosis and/or medical attention.

- The author advises readers to take full responsibility for their safety and know their limits. The author does not take any responsibility for anybody who misuses this advice.

If you think you may be suffering from any medical condition, worsening of symptoms or any new symptoms that are not resolving, you should seek immediate medical attention and insist symptoms are investigated by tests that are beyond the scope of this book.

Please use this book responsibly.

You should *never* delay seeking medical advice, disregard medical advice, or discontinue medical treatment because of the information presented in this or any other book.

DEDICATION

I dedicate this cookbook to my two wonderful children;
Maxine and Sebastian.

Doctors repeatedly told me over many years I would
never have any children so I feel very blessed and marvel
at the fine people they have become.

Maxine & Sebastian; you are both my light and my
great inspiration in the world.

Keep eating healthily, chew thoroughly and
let food be your medicine!

I love you both so much,
All my love always,

Mummy xx

ACKNOWLEDGEMENTS

I would like to say a *huge* thank you to the wonderful Christian Fioravanti for his unwavering kindness, guidance and support over the past 12 months.

Christian has been instrumental in helping me to share my Heal Endometriosis Naturally story and journey to many women around the world who are suffering with Endometriosis.

Already The Heal Endometriosis Naturally paperback book and 12 Week Program are helping to change women's lives.

Christian; you have been such an incredible star!

Thank you for all the work you do; I could not have done it without you.

Warmest regards

"The natural healing force within each one of us is the greatest force for getting well.

Our food should be our medicine. Our medicine should be our food."

- HIPPOCRATES (460-375 BC)

SPECIAL MENTIONS

Well done to Jessica Le Gray and Rachel Sledge for winning a place for their 2 recipes on Page 83 and Page 110 in this book.

Jessica and Rachel were successful participants of my Heal Endometriosis Naturally 12 Week Pilot Foundation Program in April 2016.

Jessica and Rachel; you have both been excellent students and a delight to teach.

Keep working the protocols and principles of healing your Endometriosis naturally.

Keep up the excellent work on yourself

- You Are Worth It!

ABOUT

Wendy K Laidlaw is an author, artist and Endometriosis counsellor living in Edinburgh, Scotland.

Wendy suffered from stage IV Endometriosis and Adenomyosis for over 33 years before finding a natural way out of the conditions.

Her passion is for 'thinking outside the box' with regards to the conventional medical treatment, and this mindset has helped her to heal herself from both chronic and debilitating conditions.

Wendy is an ardent promotor of what worked for her and is now eager to give hope to other millions of women who continue to needlessly suffer from Endometriosis.

Wendy loves to spend her spare time oil painting flowers and landscapes, making couture jams, completing her Psychology & Counselling Degree, playing golf and walking up The Pentland Hills with her chocolate labrador, Ginty and her two children Maxine and Sebastian.

MY STORY

For 33 years I suffered the unique, chronic and debilitating pain of Stage IV Endometriosis. It dominated and controlled my world to the point I had no life. For three decades I tried the 'usual' ways of healing myself suggested by doctors and consultants. However, the Western medical approach of using painkillers, drugs and surgery made me increasingly ill. I ended up bedridden for over 2 years; in daily debilitating and excruciating pain.

However, after retraining in a few areas (from my bed) I managed to find a natural way to heal my Endometriosis (and Adenomyosis). You can read more about my journey and the step by step approach I used in my book *'Heal Endometriosis Naturally Without Painkillers, Drugs or Surgery'.* It is important to repeat that my process is a multi-model and holistic approach; encompassing the whole body/brain connection. And it is NOT a 'quick fix'. It was necessary for me to adjust the relationship I had with my body and make necessary changes to my lifestyle. Although those changes were difficult to make at times, it was worth it.

Some people talk about the 'Endometriosis Diet', however diets are not only conflicting in advice but often are just a passing fad. Diets do not help you understand food itself or your body's mechanisms and organ systems. Diets often fail to give the necessary long term approach to your daily eating habits. What I hope to share with you in this book is an easy way to incorporate good, simple food into your body. Your body is *always* wanting to heal itself and it needs healthy nutritious foods to assist in the natural process.

My food philosophy is to think and eat in the way our hunter/gatherer ancestors of the Stone Age times would have eaten. Stay away from food s contained in plastics; Genetically Modified Foods (GMO's) which have pesticides and chemicals sprayed on them; and animal foods that have had Antibiotics and hormones injected into them.

Every thing you eat directly affects your body. Toxins and poisons have to be excreted and 'cleaned' out of your body by an overladen liver. The Stone Age lifestyle would have been free from processed foods, sugar, soy and grains. Our aim is to eat free range, hormone free, grass fed and organic foods wherever possible.

I want to encourage you to eat simply and to cook tasty, yet easy to prepare recipes for yourself, the busy endometriosis woman. Your health depends upon it...

Let food be your medicine and feel the difference in your body!

Enjoy!

Wendy xx

CONTENTS

ABOUT 11

MY STORY 12

MY FOOD PHILOSOPHY 17

THE FOOD GUIDELINES 19

EATING THE RIGHT FOODS IN ORDER - FOOD COMBINING ... 23

REMOVE & REPLACE FOR THE NEXT 12 WEEKS ... 25

SHOPPING LIST 29

BREAKFASTS 35

LUNCH & SALADS 65

MAIN 75

SMOOTHIES & JUICES 151

PUDDING 163

MY FOOD PHILOSOPHY

Keeping It Simple

The food philosophy of Healing Endometriosis Naturally consists of a few simple guidelines. Follow them and within 3-4 months you will start to feel the difference.

My philosophy is to ask yourself "Is this food something my Great Grandmother would have recognised as food?" or "How did my cave women/hunter/gatherer ancestors eat?"

You are wanting to avoid the microwave, plastics and preservatives.

I am not a fan of 'diets'. The word diet is emotive and insinuates that this eating regime is only temporary, perhaps to lose weight, and then reverts back to old ways.

This is a plan for life; this is part of your new lifestyle.

Embrace these new way of eating that I prefer to call 'Good Food Habits'.

Habits take time to develop; some say it takes 21 days to make a new habit and to break old ones. Start slowly by changing one meal a day and then increase thereafter. It is much easier to start slowly and build up from there. Slow is fast!

Please do not get fixated on calories or weight. You will be surprised that the more healthy fresh food you eat, the more your body will get healthier and stronger.

THE FOOD GUIDELINES

Guide Number One

Eat As Much As You Like Of The Right Foods

Keeping it simple means eating the 'right foods' that grow from the Earth and as close to its original sources as possible.

These foods are free from pesticides, chemicals and sprays - and of course no genetically modified foods (GMO's). You are looking for organic form - seasonal fruits, vegetables, raw nuts, seeds, sprouted seeds, beans and pulses.

You are also looking for organic, free range, hormone free meats and chicken, and fresh caught (not farmed) fish.

Guide Number Two

Dump The Junk & Plastics

Junk food is high in sugar which releases endorphins and dopamine ('the feel good' hormone) - hence why they feel good temporarily. However, within a short while the sugar slump kicks in and you may feel flat; and pain is ignited.

Guide Number Three

Never Go Hungry!

Eat little and often which will help blood sugar levels be balanced and maintain energy throughout the day.

Guide Number Four

Sit Down To Eat

Sit down and spend a *minimum* of 30 minutes for each meal time. Eating on the run or standing up makes the digestive process harder causing heartburn, indigestion and bloated stomach.

Guide Number Five

Chew, Chew, Chew Your Food; 15-20 Times Each Mouthful

Your stomach does not have teeth! Flatulence and bloated stomaches happen when you have undigested food particles in the small intestine. Teeth used for chewing, which is also called mastication and the chewing action help to stimulate the digestive process by releasing digestive enzymes

Guide Number Six

Get Creative

Experiment and get in touch with your creativity. Alternate some ingredients in some of the recipes or dishes to add variety to your new heathy eating habits.

Guide Number Seven

Fail to Plan, Plan to Fail

If you are a busy working women or laid up in bed in chronic pain then the idea of shopping, preparing, cooking and then eating food may feel overwhelming. So make sure you plan in advance. Use the many wonderful resources that are averrable online. Many companies will deliver a box full of every ingredient you need to make a delicious healthy meal to your front door.

THE FOOD GUIDELINES

Guide Number Eight

Food And Emotions

I believe that our body, our emotions and what we eat are all intricately linked - as each affects the other. Be more aware and perceptive of how you feel after eating certain foods. I would suggest keeping a food journal to monitor. Notice if there any patterns.

Guide Number Nine

You Are What You Digest

According to studies 50 percent of the Western population have insufficient stomach acid; a condition call Hypochlorhydria. You can do a simple home baking soda test to check your stomach acid. If it is low then supplement with betaine HCL with every meal. I would also suggest digestive enzymes are taken with every meal to assist with the break down of foods.

Guide Number Ten

Give It 12 Weeks Minimum

Make the commitment to yourself and your body for the next 12 weeks to eat fresh, organic, free range, hormone free, and grass fed foods. Avoid food in plastic containers or wrapping and stay away from using the microwave. No exceptions. After 12 weeks introduce a 90/10 approach; do what I suggest for 90 percent of the time and you can indulge with less healthy treats 10 percent of the time. Once you are reintroduced to healthy great tasting food, you may not have the desire to indulge in processed sugar food. You may never look back!

EATING THE RIGHT FOODS IN ORDER - FOOD COMBINING

If you have tested your stomach acid levels and are supplementing with digestive enzymes but you are still experiencing gas and bloating, you may wish to consider the food combining approach; for example make sure you separate the food groups during eating; see guideline below.

Digestive Processing

Fruit	quickest	30 minutes
Carbohydrates	medium	60 minutes
Protein	longest	90 minutes

Always eat fruit 30 minutes before any other food types.

Leave two hours after a carbohydrate based meal before eating a dense protein meal

Leave three hours before eating carbohydrates, after eating solid protein

Beans and pulses are combination of protein and starch, so are easily combined into salads.

Good Food V Bad Food

Organic Foods

Organic food means food that is free of pesticides and has not been sprayed with chemical fertilisers. Chemically treated soils and chemicals sprayed on the produce are toxic to your body cells and bloodstream.

REMOVE & REPLACE FOR THE NEXT 12 WEEKS

REMOVE:

For the next 12 weeks please remove the following foods from your daily food habits;

Wheat flour
Gluten
Margarine
Artificial Sugar
Artificial Sweeteners
Alcohol/Beer/Lager
Coffee
Cows Milk
Corn
Processed Foods
Microwave Meals
Soy/Soya

"There is no sincerer love than the love of food."

– GEORGE BERNARD SHAW

REPLACE:

For the next 12 weeks please replace the
above with the following foods;

Wheat/Gluten FREE Rice Flour
Full Fat Organic Butter
Natural Sugars
Mineral Water
Herbal/Fruit Teas
Goats or Ewes Milk
Coconut Milk/Water (no sugar)
Fresh,
Organic,
Free range,
Hormone FREE meats

REMOVE AND REPLACE

*"We all eat, and it would be a sad waste
of opportunity to eat badly."*

-ANNA THOMAS

SHOPPING LIST

Here is an 'ideal' shopping list to help you get started on the path to healing your Endometriosis naturally. Swap out food items as you deplete them so then you only have great foods in your cupboards.

Some items may not be available in supermarkets so check out farmer's markets, local health food stores, go online or search locally to see what is in season.

Always Go Certified Organic!

Make sure you purchase organic vegetables and fruit produce for every meal. Ensure you buy free range organic eggs, with all meat or chicken being free range, hormone free and grass fed. This is essential to give your body a break from the toxins and avoid pesticides, chemicals and fertilisers. Avoid all Genetically Modified Foods (GMO's), foods with any preservatives, colourings or additives.

Aim to have at least 6-7 vegetables and one piece of fruit a day. Juicing vegetables is a great way to help increase consumption.

LEAFY GREEN VEGETABLES

Kale
Chicory
Spinach
Collard greens
Swiss chard
Mustard greens
Broccoli rabe
Beet greens
Dandelion greens
Arugula
Red/Green leaf lettuce
Romaine lettuce
Iceberg lettuce
Turnip greens

Parsley
Watercress
Rocket

Cruciferous Vegetables
Bok choy
Purple sprouting broccoli
Romanesco broccoli
Broccolini
Brussels sprouts
Cabbage (purple)
Chinese cabbage
Cauliflower
Purple cauliflower
Chinese cabbage
Turnips
Celeriac

SWEET VEGETABLES

Sweet potatoes
Beetroots
Pumpkin
Acorn squash
Butternut squash
Spaghetti squash
Parsnip
Carrots

OTHER VEGETABLES

Asparagus
Brown Onions
Red Onions
Garlic
Fennel
Leeks
Celery
Zucchini
Cucumbers
Tomatoes
Bell peppers
Snap peas
Courgette
Artichoke
Yam

GRAINS

Rice Flour
Potato Flour
Almond Flour
Quinoa (in moderation)
Millet
Short grain brown rice (non GMO)
Long grain brown rice (non GMO)
Brown basmati rice
Gluten-free steel-cut oats
Buckwheat (aka kash)

BEANS

Aduki beans
Kidney beans
Lentils (all colours)
White beans
Garbanzo beans
Black beans
Split peas
Lima beans
Pinto beans
Chickpeas

SEEDS & RAW NUTS

Pumpkin seeds
Pecan Nuts
Sunflower seeds
Almonds
Walnuts
Pistachio
Cashews
Brazil nuts
Chia seeds
Sesame seeds
Hazelnuts
Chestnuts
Pinenuts

SHOPPING LIST

FRUITS

Strawberries
Blackberries
Blueberries
Raspberries
Goji berries
Cherries
Kiwi
Pears
Apples
Lemons
Olives
Cranberries
Plums
Melons
Grapefruit
Avocado

SPICES

Turmeric
Saffron
Bay leaf
Thyme
Sage
Rosemary
Dill
Fennel
Cumin
Basil
Cayennepepper
Caraway Mustard seeds
Cardamom
Cilantro

FATS, OILS & BUTTERS

Organic coconut oil
Organic cold pressed coconut butter
Organic cold-pressed olive oil
Almond butter
Peanut butter (unsweetened)

CONDIMENTS

Tamari (gluten free)
Olives
Kimchi
Good quality sea salt
Rock salt
Black pepper
Balsamic vinegar
Apple cider vinegar
Natural organic mustard
Organic sauerkraut
Fresh ginger
Fresh garlic
Fresh parsley

FRESH FISH

Wild caught salmon
Cod
Haddock
Trout
Mackerel
Herring
Sardines

SHOPPING LIST

ANIMAL PROTEIN

Free-range grass fed,
hormone-free beef
Free-range grass fed,
hormone-free pork
Free-range grass fed,
hormone-free lamb
Free-range organic veal
Free-range organic turkey
Free-range organic chicken
(not corn fed)
Duck
Pheasant
Venison

BEVERAGES & REFRESHMENTS

Rooibos/redbush tea
Red raspberry leaf tea
Lemon tea
Dandelion root tea
Japanese kukicha tea/
green
twig tea
Peppermint tea
Chamomile tea
Jasmine tea
Green tea
Nettle tea
Dill tea

DAIRY SUBSTITUTES

Coconut milk
Almond milk
Oat milk
Rice milk
Hemp milk
Goats milk

NATURAL SWEETENERS

Manuka honey
Raw honeycomb
Agar syrup
Rice syrup
D-ribose

SHOPPING LIST

BREAKFAST LIKE A KING OR A QUEEN!

Breakfast is the MOST important meal of the day and 'breaks' the fast of the night.

Fill up your body as you would fill up the tank of a car with petrol. Remember you cannot run on empty and to do so will add great stress to an inflamed body if you do.

Always eat within one hour of waking.

If you are not a morning person, and struggle to eat, then try to 'drink' your breakfast. Consider making a homemade Power Protein Shake for the ultimate start to your day. Purchase some organic rice protein powder and multi-vitamin powder drink (wheat grass free) to have in addition to your breakfast meal for extra energy.

"Probably one of the most private things in the world is an egg until it is broken."

MFK FISHER

BOILED FREE RANGE ORGANIC EGGS WITH CHOPPED BASIL

INGREDIENTS:

2 free range organic eggs
1 tsp of chopped basil
Black pepper

METHOD:

1. Add the free range, organic eggs to a pot of boiling water. Be very gentle while doing this to prevent the free range organic eggs from cracking.

   (Top tip; to prepare the perfect free range organic eggs is to add 1 tbs of baking soda into the boiling water. This will make a peeling process much easier.)

2. Boil the free range organic eggs for 8 minutes. You can use a kitchen timer, or simply your watch. After 8 minutes, drain the water and place the free range organic eggs under the cold water for few minutes. Peel and slice the free range organic eggs. Sprinkle with chopped basil and serve.

"If you're afraid of butter, use cream."

~ JULIA CHILD

BREAKFAST

PINEAPPLE OMELETTE WITH ALMONDS

INGREDIENTS:

3 thick slices of pineapple, peeled
2 free range organic eggs
½ cup of almonds, minced
1 tbs of coconut oil for frying
½ tsp of salt

METHOD:

Break the free range organic eggs into a bowl and beat well until combined. Add minced almonds and mix well. Season with salt. Heat up the coconut oil in a large saucepan, over a medium temperature. First you want to fry pineapple slices for about 2-3 minutes on each side, until a golden brown colour. Reduce the heat to low. Pour egg mixture into pan and fry for a few more minutes, stirring constantly. Remove from the heat and enjoy.

"First we eat, then we
do everything else."

-M.F.K. FISHER

TROPICAL FRUIT SALAD

INGREDIENTS:

1 cup of berries

½ cup of pineapple cubes

½ cup of chopped apple

5 mint springs

1 tbs of fresh lime juice

1 tsp of lime zest

¼ cup of water

1 tsp of cinnamon

METHOD:

1. In a small saucepan combine ¼ cup of water, mint spring, fresh lime juice and lime zest. Allow it to boil over medium temperature and cook for about approximately 2-3 minutes. Remove from the heat and leave to cool.

2. Meanwhile, in a large bowl, combine 1 cup of berries, ½ cup of pineapple cubes and ½ cup of chopped apple. Pour the lime mixture over the salad and let it stand in the refrigerator for 20-30 minutes. Remove from the refrigerator and sprinkle with 1 tsp of cinnamon before serving. This can be done the night before.

"Don't eat anything your Great-Grandmother wouldn't recognise as food."

~ MICHAEL POLLAN

BREAKFAST

PLUM BREAKFAST CAKE

INGREDIENTS:

1 cup of almond flour

2 tbs of rice flour

1 tsp of baking soda

2 tsp of sugar free vanilla extract

2 tbs of coconut oil

2 free range organic eggs

⅓ cup of plums, finely chopped

⅓ cup of almonds, minced

1 tsp of cinnamon

METHOD:

1. For the dough, mix together almond flour, rice flour, baking soda and vanilla extract. Add the free range organic eggs and coconut oil. Whisk together until a smooth mixture, then set aside.

2. In another bowl, combine the plums, minced almonds and cinnamon. Stir well.

3. Transfer the dough onto a baking sheet. Sprinkle with the plum mixture and roll the dough into a long rectangle. Cut into 7 equal pieces and let it stand in the refrigerator for approximately 20 minutes before baking.

4. Meanwhile, preheat the oven to 325 degrees. Bake for approximately 10 minutes, or until nice golden colour. Serve warm.

BREAKFAST

GRILLED EGGPLANT/AUBERGINE SLICES WITH CHOPPED FENNEL

INGREDIENTS:

1 large Eggplant/Aubergine

½ cup of chopped fennel

1 tbs of olive oil

1 tsp of chopped parsley

METHOD:

Peel the Eggplant/Aubergine and cut into 3 equal slices. Bake it in a barbecue pan with coconut oil. When done, spread olive oil over it, and sprinkle with fennel and parsley.

(These Eggplant/Aubergine slices are also great cold, so you can leave them overnight in a refrigerator).

SPINACH OMELETTE

INGREDIENTS:

1 cup of chopped spinach
2 free range organic eggs
1 tbs of coconut oil for frying
1 tsp of fresh parsley, chopped

METHOD:

Heat up the coconut oil over a medium temperature. stirring constantly, gently cook the spinach until mostly wilted, This should take no more than 5 minutes. Remove from the heat and set pan aside. Beat the free range organic eggs using a fork and pour over spinach. Return the pan to the heat and stir well for about a minute and add chopped parsley.

NUTMEG OMELETTE

INGREDIENTS:

3 free range organic eggs

1 medium onion

2 tbs of coconut oil

1 tsp of nutmeg

1/5 tsp of pepper

METHOD:

Peel and slice the onion. Wash under the cool water and drain. Set aside. Heat the coconut oil in a nonstick frying pan over a medium heat. In a small bowl, whisk together free range organic eggs and pepper. Pour the free range organic eggs in a frying pan and fry for about 3 minutes. Using a spatula, remove the free range organic eggs from the frying pan and add onions and nutmeg. Stir well and return the free range organic eggs to the frying pan. Cook for few more minutes, until the onions are a golden colour.

BANANA DELIGHT

INGREDIENTS:

1 large organic banana

2 free range egg whites

1.5 cups of water

1 tsp of ground vanilla extract

METHOD:

Peel and chop the banana into small cubes. Combine with other ingredients in a blender and mix for 30 seconds, until a smooth mixture. Keep in the refrigerator and serve cold.(You could also add organic vanilla rice protein powder for extra boost).

BREAKFAST

Why not go out on a limb? Isn't that where the fruit is?"

~ FRANK SCULLY

BANANA LOAF BREAD

INGREDIENTS

2 cups of wheat free/gluten free flour

1 tsp bicarbonate of soda

½ tsp salt

4oz organic coconut butter

1 half cup of coconut milk

2 free range organic eggs

4 ripe bananas, mashed

1 tsp vanilla extract

METHOD

1. Sift the flour, bicarbonate of soda and salt into a large mixing bowl.

2. In a separate bowl, cream the coconut butter, add the free range organic eggs, mashed bananas, coconut milk and vanilla extract mixture. Mix well until light and fluffy. Fold in the flour. Grease a 20cm x 12.5cm/8in x 5in loaf tin and pour the cake mixture into the tin. Transfer to the oven and bake for about an hour at 300 C, or until well-risen and golden-brown. Remove from the oven and leave to cool in the tin for a few minutes, then place onto a wire rack to cool completely before serving.

BREAKFAST

49

ALMOND & AVOCADO BREAKFAST MUFFINS

INGREDIENTS:

½ cup of almond flour

¼ cup of coconut flour

½ tsp of baking soda

½ tsp of cinnamon

½ tsp of nutmeg

1 medium avocado, sliced

2 free range organic eggs

1½ tsp of vanilla extract

1 tbs of coconut oil

½ cup of almond milk

METHOD:

Preheat the oven to 300 C. In a large bowl, combine the almond flour, coconut flour, baking soda, cinnamon, and nutmeg. In a small bowl, combine free range organic eggs, avocado slices, coconut oil and almond milk. Pour this mixture into a blender and mix well for about 30 seconds. Now combine both mixtures using an electric mixer. Pour into muffin moulds and bake for about 20 minutes. Remove from the oven and allow it to cool before eating.

"All happiness depends on a leisurely breakfast."

-JOHN GUNTHER

BREAKFAST

SCRAMBLED FREE RANGE ORGANIC EGGS WITH CHOPPED MINT

INGREDIENTS:

3 free range organic eggs

1 tbs of coconut oil

1 tbs of chopped mint

1 cup of cherry tomatoes

1 small onion

salt and pepper to taste

METHOD:

Cut the vegetables into small pieces and fry in a large saucepan over a low temperature for about 15 minutes. Wait for the water to evaporate. Beat the free range organic eggs and add chopped mint. Mix with the tomatoes and onion, add coconut oil and fry for a few minutes. Before serving add some rock salt and pepper to taste.

"Cooking well doesn't mean cooking fancy"

– WENDY K LAIDLAW

BREAKFAST

MIXED BERRIES PANCAKES

INGREDIENTS:

3 free range organic eggs

½ cup coconut flour

½ cup almond flour

1 cup of coconut milk

1 tsp of apple vinegar

1 tsp vanilla essence

½ tsp of baking soda

¼ tsp salt

coconut oil for frying

3 cups of mixed fresh berries

Agave Syrup

METHOD:

1. In a large bowl, combine the coconut flour, almond flour, vanilla, baking soda, and salt. In a smaller bowl, mix coconut milk and apple vinegar. Whisk ingredients until they are a smooth dough.

2. Using a nonstick frying pan, heat up the coconut oil over a medium heat. Spread the desired amount of dough over the frying pan. Use a spoon to smooth the surface of each pancake. Fry for about 2-3 minutes on each side. Top with mixed fresh berries and 1 tbs of agave syrup.

BREAKFAST

ROSEMARY BREAKFAST BISCUITS

INGREDIENTS:

1 cup of almond or rice flour

¼ cup of coconut flour

1 tsp of rosemary powder, organic

1 tsp of dried rosemary, crushed

1 tbs of coconut flour

1 cup of coconut milk

3 free range organic free range organic eggs

½ cup of water

METHOD:

1. Preheat the oven to 350 C. Line a baking tin with some baking paper and set aside.

2. Combine all dry ingredients, except the eggs, water and coconut milk, in a bowl and stir well. Then whisk in eggs, water, and coconut milk and whisk until thoroughly combined. Shape biscuits with your hands, or use a biscuit mould and place on baking tin. Transfer to the oven and bake for 15-20 minutes.

"The only real stumbling block is fear of failure. In cooking you've got to have a what-the-hell attitude."

~ JULIA CHILD

MUSHROOM OMELETTE

INGREDIENTS:

1 cup of button mushrooms, sliced

2 free range organic eggs

1 tsp of fresh rosemary, chopped

¼ tsp of dry oregano

1 tbs of coconut oil

METHOD:

1. Heat up the coconut oil in a large frying pan, over a medium temperature. Add the sliced button mushrooms and cook for 3-4 minutes ,until the water evaporates. Remove from the frying pan and place to the side.

2. In a small bowl, whisk together free range organic eggs, rosemary and oregano. Pour the mixture in the frying pan and fry for about 4 minutes. When the free range organic eggs are set, layer half of the frying pan with mushrooms. Fold the untopped half of the omelette over filling and fry 1 minute. Move to a plate and serve with few lettuce leaves (optional).

BREAKFAST

AVOCADO FREE RANGE ORGANIC EGGS

INGREDIENTS:

4 free range organic eggs

1 cup of avocado puree, organic

1 tbs of coconut oil

1 large tomato, roughly chopped

1 large onion, peeled and finely chopped

1 tbs of minced hazelnuts

1 tbs of lemon juice

Rock or sea salt

METHOD:

1. Boil the free range organic eggs in water for 5 minutes. (Top tip; add 1 tsp of baking soda into the boiling water which makes the peeling process much easier.) Drain and place the free range organic eggs under cold water for 2 minutes. Peel and cut into small pieces.

2. Place 1 cup of avocado puree and 1 tbs of coconut oil in a food processor. Mix well for 30 seconds. Combine the free range organic eggs with chopped tomato, sliced onion, and hazelnuts in a separate bowl. Whisk in avocado mixture and mix well. Add 1 tbs of lemon juice and some salt to taste. Serve cold.

"A balanced diet is a (wheat/ gluten/ sugar free) cookie in each hand."

-BARBARA JOHNSON

where?

ALMOND PANCAKES

coconut

INGREDIENTS:

1 cup of coconut flour
1 tbs of baking soda
2 free range organic eggs
1 cup of coconut milk
½ cup of water
sea salt
cinnamon to taste
1 tbs of coconut oil

METHOD:

Combine all dry ingredients with coconut milk and water. Mix well to make a smooth dough. Add some cinnamon to taste and fry over a medium heat for about 3-4 minutes on each side. These pancakes are perfect with strawberries or other fruits on top.

COCONUT MUFFINS

INGREDIENTS:

1 cup of almond flour
¼ cup of coconut flour
¼ tsp of baking soda
½ cup of coconut milk
2 tbs of coconut oil
2 free range organic eggs
½ cup of fresh raspberries

METHOD:

1. Preheat the oven to 300 C.

2. In a large bowl, combine all dry ingredients and mix well. In a separate bowl, whisk together coconut milk, coconut oil, and free range organic eggs. Gently combine these two mixtures and add the raspberries. Spread the mixture into muffin moulds and bake for about 20 minutes.

COCONUT BREAKFAST BREAD

INGREDIENTS:

1 cup of almond or rice flour

1 tsp of baking soda

2 large bananas

1 cup of Brazil nuts, minced

2 tbs of coconut oil

2 free range organic eggs

1 tsp of sugar free vanilla extract

½ tsp of cinnamon

FOR THE FILLING:

2 free range organic eggs

⅓ cup of coconut milk

1 tsp of sugar free vanilla extract

¼ teaspoon of cinnamon

1 tbs of coconut oil

METHOD:

1. Preheat oven to 350 C.

2. Using an electric mixer, combine the Brazil nuts and coconut oil until you get a smooth butter mixture.

3. Peel the bananas and chop them roughly. Add coconut mixture and banana slices into a food processor and combine for about a minute.

4. Combine almond flour, baking soda, vanilla extract and cinnamon in a large bowl. Whisk in the free range organic eggs and banana mixture, making a smooth dough.

5. Spread the dough over a small baking sheet (the size depends on how thick you want your bread to be). Place in the oven and bake for about 25 minutes, or until a light brown colour. Remove from the oven and allow it to cool.

6. Cut the bread into 1-inch slices. Set aside.

BREAKFAST

FOR THE FILLING;

In a smaller bowl, combine the free range organic eggs, coconut milk, vanilla extract and cinnamon. Use a large, nonstick frying pan to heat up 1 tbs of coconut oil, over a medium temperature. Dip the bread slices in your egg mixture and fry for abut 2 minutes on each side. Use kitchen paper to remove the excess oil and serve.

"When baking, follow directions. When cooking, go by your own taste."

~ LAIKO BAHRS

LUNCH & SALADS

The act of putting into your mouth what the earth has grown is perhaps your most direct interaction with the earth."

~ FRANCES MOORE LAPPE

GREEN TUNA SALAD

INGREDIENTS:

1 cup of tuna

½ cup of green beans, cooked

2 cups of chopped lettuce

1 cup of cherry tomatoes, cut in half

1 small red onion, peeled and sliced

2 dry basil leaves, crushed

2 free range organic eggs, boiled

4 tbss of coconut oil

¼ tsp of black pepper, ground

1 tbs of fresh lemon juice

1 tbs of water

2 garlic cloves, crushed

2 tsps of capers

METHOD:

1. Pour 3 cups of water in a pot and bring it to boil. Add beans and cook until tender. This should take about 15 minutes. Remove from the heat and drain. Meanwhile, boil the free range organic eggs for 10 minutes. Remove from the boiling water and allow your free range organic eggs to cool for a while. Meanwhile, in a large bowl, combine the salad ingredients – tuna, green beans, chopped lettuce, cherry tomatoes and onions. Peel the free range organic eggs and add to your salad.

2. In another, smaller bowl, combine the coconut oil, basil leaves, black pepper, lemon juice, water, crushed garlic cloves and capers. Mix the ingredients until well combined. Pour this mixture evenly over your tuna salad and chill in the refrigerator for 30 minutes before serving.

LUNCH & SALADS

FETA GOATS CHEESE SALAD

INGREDIENTS:

200 grams of feta goats cheese

1 cup of chopped salad leaves

1 large tomato

1 small onion

1 tbs of ground garlic

1 tbs of lemon juice

Rock salt and black pepper
   to taste

METHOD:

1. Wash and cut the vegetables. Combine the ingredients in a large bowl and season with lemon juice, salt and pepper.

2. You can also add some chilli, curry, turmeric or ginger, depending on your taste (optional).

Learn how to cook-try new recipes, learn from your mistakes, be fearless, and above all have fun!'

~ JULIA CHILD

SPANISH CHICKEN MIX SALAD

INGREDIENTS:

3 free range organic eggs

2 cups of chopped skinless free range organic chicken breast

1 organic red pepper

1 tsp of ground dry rosemary

coconut oil for frying

¼ tsp of pepper

FOR THE SALAD:

1 cup of chopped lettuce

½ cup of steamed broccoli

6 cherry tomatoes

¼ cup of coconuts

1 tbs of coconut oil

1 tbs of lemon juice

Rock or sea salt

METHOD:

1. Firstly, prepare the free range organic eggs. Using a large saucepan and add some coconut oil to it and fry the chicken over a medium temperature for about 15-20 minutes, stirring constantly, until nicely golden brown colour. Add chopped red pepper and stir well. Meanwhile, beat the free range organic eggs in a bowl and add the rosemary. Mix with the chicken and red pepper in a saucepan and fry for few more minutes. Remove from the heat and allow it to cool for 10 minutes.

2. Combine the lettuce, steamed broccoli and tomatoes in a large bowl. Add coconuts and egg mixture. Mix well with a fork and season with coconut oil and lemon juice. Add some salt to taste.

GRILLED RED PEPPER & FETA GOATS CHEESE

INGREDIENTS:

200 grams of feta goats cheese, crumbled

3 large organic red bell peppers

3 tbs of coconut oil

3 cloves of garlic

2 tbs of chopped parsley

METHOD:

Heat up the grill pan over a medium temperature. Mix the coconut oil with garlic and parsley in a small bowl. Cut the peppers in half, fill with feta cheese and, rub the coconut oil on each piece. Place in a grill pan, skin-side up, and grill until the skin blackens.

APPLE CINNAMON SALAD

INGREDIENTS:

4 organic Red Delicious apples, cored and sliced

1 Granny Smith apple, cored and diced

½ cup of chopped celery

1 pear, peeled and diced

½ cup seedless grapes

½ cup of grated carrot

1 lemon sliced

Cinnamon

Coconut sugar

METHOD:

Once you have all of the above ingredients are sliced, cut and measured out, add all of them to a large bowl. Squeeze a small amount of lemon juice over the fruit. This can be served with a leafy salad and/or topped with a little cinnamon and coconut sugar.

LUNCH & SALADS

PEPERONATA & TOMATOES

INGREDIENTS:

2 tbs of coconut oil
1 small onion, sliced
2 cloves of garlic, chopped
1 organic red pepper chopped
2 organic small tomatoes, sliced
1 tbs of apple vinegar
2 tbs of coconut oil
Basil leaves for decoration
Rock salt and black pepper

METHOD:

1. Heat up the coconut oil in a large saucepan over a medium heat. Add sliced onion and fry until golden colour. Add the garlic and red pepper, then season with salt and black pepper. Fry for 15 minutes, stirring constantly.

2. Reduce the heat to low and add the tomatoes. Cover and cook for 2-3 minutes. Remove from the heat and serve as a delicious main or side dish. To finish add the basil leaves for both a flavoursome and decorative flare.

MEDITERRANEAN MACKEREL SALAD

INGREDIENTS:

3 mackerel fillets, without bones

1 cup of organic cherry tomatoes

1 cup of organic tender stem broccoli

1 tsp of ground rosemary

1 tsp of ground garlic

1 tsp of ground basil

2 tbs of lemon juice

Coconut oil for frying

Rock or sea salt

METHOD:

Sprinkle the mackerel fillets with rosemary and fry in a large saucepan at 350 C for about 10 minutes on each side, until a nice golden colour. Use kitchen paper to soak up the excess oil. Allow the fillets to cool for about 15 minutes. Put broccoli into seasoned cold water, bring to the boil and take off and drain. Mix the fish with other ingredients on a large plate. Add garlic, basil and lemon juice. Add a pinch of salt and serve warm.

CARROT & CINNAMON STICKS

INGREDIENTS:

10 organic carrots
1 tbs of coconut oil
1 tsp of ground cinnamon

METHOD:

Peel and wash your carrots and cut into 4 lengths. Preheat the oven to 450 C.

Combine coconut oil with cinnamon. Brush this mixture over your carrots.

Transfer to the baking sheet and cook for 30 minutes. Serve warm.

If organic farming is the natural way, shouldn't organic produce just be called "produce" and make the pesticide-laden stuff take the burden of an adjective?"

~ YMBER DELECTO

LUNCH & SALADS

MAINS

You could probably get through life without knowing how to roast a chicken, but the question is, would you want to?"

~ NIGELLA LAWSON

TASTY CHICKEN CURRY

INGREDIENTS:

1 cup of organic skinless chicken fillets, chopped

4 organic carrots, chopped

3 tbs of coconut oil

2 tbs of ginger, freshly chopped

2 garlic cloves, crushed

5 scallions onions, diced

4 cups of chicken stock

1 tbs of curry powder

salt to taste

ground pepper to taste

squeeze of lime

METHOD:

Heat the oil over a medium heat in a saucepan. Stir in crushed garlic, scallions onions and ginger, until soft. Add the remaining ingredients, stir and bring to the boil. Reduce the heat to low, cover and let it simmer for about 20 minutes until the chicken becomes tender. Pour into bowls and serve.

MAINS

CRUSTLESS QUICHE

INGREDIENTS:

4 free range organic eggs

¼ cup of almond or rice flour

1 tbs of almond butter

2 cups of coconut milk

1 small onion, chopped

4 large slices of free range bacon

1 tbs of dry parsley, chopped

½ tsp of salt

¼ tsp of pepper

METHOD:

In a large bowl, whisk together the free range organic eggs and coconut milk. Add the almond or rice flour and butter. Mix well with an electric mixer until it is a smooth batter. Add other ingredients and pour this mixture into a flan baking dish. Preheat the oven to 300 C and bake for about 30 minutes.

CARROT PATÈ

INGREDIENTS:

½ cup of canned/organic carrots, cooked and chopped

¼ cup of sweet potato puree, canned

½ cup of coconut cream

3-4 cloves of garlic, chopped

¼ cup of coconut milk

1 tbs of mustard

¼ tsp of salt

METHOD:

Mix together the garlic and mustard. In a large bowl, combine coconut cream with coconut milk, salt, canned carrots and sweet potato puree. Mix well and add the garlic and mustard. Allow it to stand in the refrigerator for about an hour before serving. You can keep it in the refrigerator for up to 10 days.

MAINS

BROCCOLI PUREE WITH GREEN PEPPERS

INGREDIENTS:

½ cup of cooked organic broccoli, pureed
2 small organic green peppers, chopped
¼ tsp of red pepper
¼ tsp of sea salt
1 tbs of coconut oil

METHOD:

1. Combine the broccoli puree with red pepper and sea salt and mix well using a fork.

2. Heat up the coconut oil over a medium to high heat and fry the chopped green peppers for about 10 minutes. Add the broccoli puree, stirring well and fry for another 3 minutes. Remove from the heat and serve.

SALMON WITH COURGETTE

INGREDIENTS:

1 lb of sliced salmon fillets

2 small courgette

6 Brussels sprouts

6 Asparagus spears

3 tbs of extra virgin coconut oil

¼ tsp of pepper

METHOD:

1. Peel and slice the courgette into 0.5-inch thick circle shaped slices. Cut salmon fillets into bite size pieces. Heat up one tbs of coconut oil in a large frying pan and add the salmon fillets. Sprinkle with black pepper and fry them for about 10 minutes, or until nice and crispy. When done, move them to a plate covered with kitchen paper to soak up the grease. Set aside.

2. Cut the Brussels sprouts in half. Combine with courgette slices in a large bowl and add the remaining 2 tbs of coconut oil. Move the vegetables to the frying pan and cook with the asparagus until the Brussel sprouts are tender. This should take no more than 10 minutes. Add your salmon fillets to the frying pan, cover and allow it to rewarm. Serve and enjoy.

MAINS

81

GRILLED ORGANIC RED PEPPER

INGREDIENTS:

1 large organic red pepper

1 tbs of coconut oil

2 cloves of garlic

Chopped parsley

METHOD:

Mix coconut oil with garlic and parsley. Spread the sauce over pepper and bake in barbecue pan at low temperature for about 10-15 minutes.

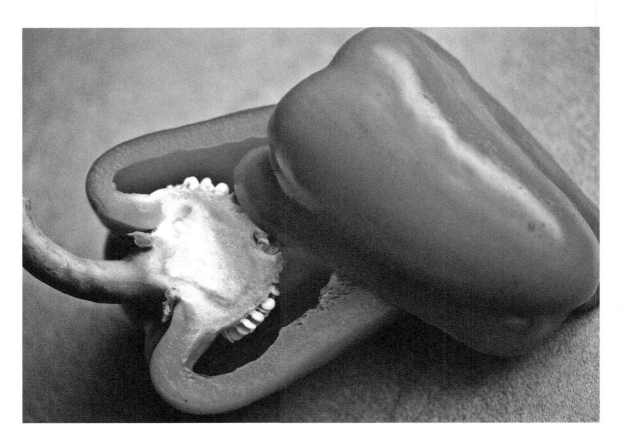

MAINS

TANGY VEGAN STUFFED PEPPERS
(by Rachel Sledge)

INGREDIENTS:

4 whole organic bell peppers
1 cup diced organic bell pepper
I cup organic zucchini
I cup organic onion
1 ½ cup lentils
I cup brown rice
2 cups sweet and spicy BBQ sauce
2 ½ cups water
I cup vegetable stock

METHOD:

1. Cut off the tops of three whole peppers, clean out the seeds and set them aside. Dice up one pepper and combine with the onion, zucchini, dried lentils, water and vegetable stock in to a large pot. Pour in the BBQ sauce. Cook on a medium heat or a crock pot on high heat for 1 hour. After 1 hour add in the brown rice and lentils. Cook for an additional 2-3 hours stirring occasional until rice and lentils are cooked.

2. Once mixture is cooked add mixture to peppers and bake at 175 C for 40-50 minutes.

(**Top Tip;** if your peppers do not stand up, add some mixture to the bottom of the baking dish).

SWEET CARROT PURÉE

INGREDIENTS:

1 large carrot, grated

2 cups of coconut yogurt

½ cup of organic sweet potato purée

1 cup of chopped lettuce

1 tbs of coconut oil

1 tsp of apple-cider vinegar

salt to taste

METHOD:

Mix the carrot, coconut yogurt and sweet potato puree in a bowl. Keep this mixture in the refrigerator for at least one hour. Remove from the fridge and add the chopped lettuce, coconut oil, and apple vinegar. Mix well and serve. Add salt to season.

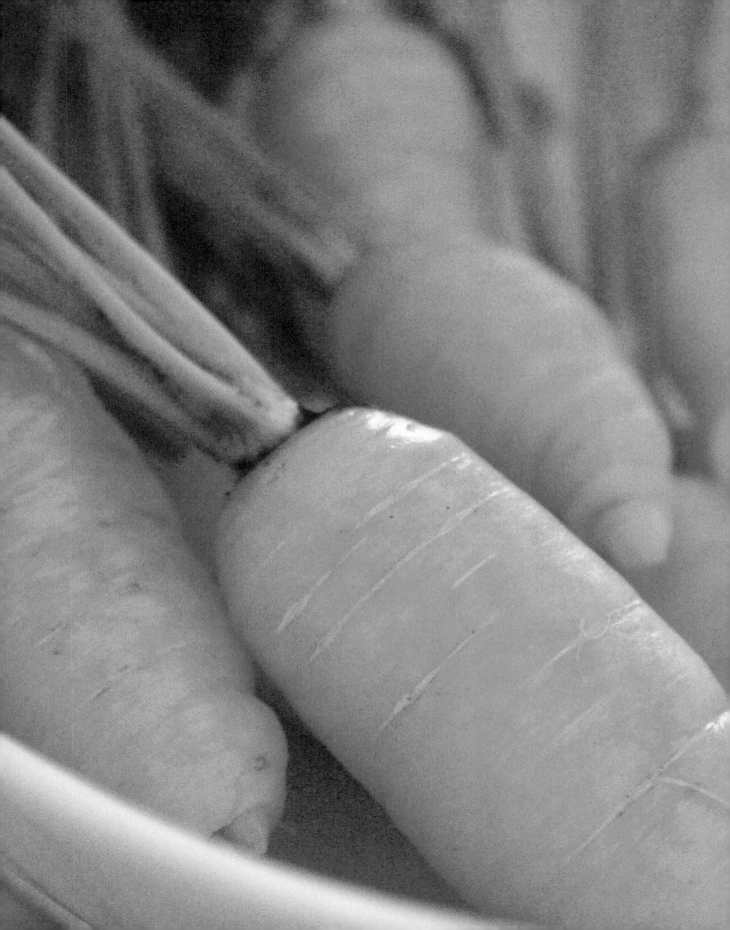

SHRIMPS IN TOMATO SAUCE

INGREDIENTS:

3 cups of frozen shrimps

3 medium tomatoes

1 tsp of dried basil

3 cloves of garlic, chopped

¼ tsp of ground black pepper

¼ cup of coconut oil

3 tbs of coconut oil for frying

METHOD:

1. Whisk together the ¼ cup of coconut oil, one tsp of dried basil, chopped garlic and ground black pepper in a bowl. Brush each shrimp with this marinade and set aside. Wash and roughly chop the tomatoes and set aside.

2. Use a large grill pan to heat up 3 tbs of coconut oil. Remove the shrimps from the marinade and grill for a few minutes on each side. You want to see a light golden brown colour on your shrimps. Reduce the heat to minimum and add the chopped tomatoes. Cover and cook until the tomatoes soften. Serve warm.

CHICKEN BALLS

INGREDIENTS:

1lb of organic free range chicken breast, boneless and skinless, minced

1 cup of almond flour

1 tsp of baking powder

3 organic free range eggs

1 cup of coconut milk

5 tbs of coconut oil

METHOD:

1. Combine all dry ingredients with the chicken. Use your hands to mix well making sure to wash them afterwards. Gently whisk in 1 cup of coconut milk, 2 tbs of coconut oil and free range organic eggs. Shape into bite sized balls.

2. Heat up the remaining 3 tbs of coconut oil in a deep saucepan. Fry for about 10 minutes, until a golden brown colour. Remove from the saucepan and place on a plate lined with some kitchen paper to soak up the excess oil. Serve warm or cold.

MAINS

GRILLED EGGPLANT/AUBERGINE WITH MINT

INGREDIENTS:

3 large Eggplant/Aubergines
1 tbs of chopped basil
½ cup of chopped fresh mint
¼ cup of extra virgin coconut oil
pepper to taste
Rock or sea salt

METHOD:

Cut each eggplant/aubergine lengthwise into five slices. Toss the eggplant/aubergine slices with some salt and leave aside for 15 minutes. Rinse well and press gently to drain and extract any excess liquid. Pat dry using kitchen paper. Whisk together coconut oil, 1 tbs of chopped basil and ¼ cup of chopped mint. Stir in some pepper to taste. Gently brush this mixture over each eggplant/aubergine slice and fry in a nonstick frying pan over a moderately high heat, for about one minute per side. Remove from the pan and use a kitchen paper to soak the excess oil. Transfer to a large and shallow dish. Next use the remaining ¼ cup of fresh mint to cover the eggplant/aubergine slices. Leave in the refrigerator overnight.

SPICED APPLE PURÉE

INGREDIENTS:

1 cup of homemade apple puree

½ cup of coconut oil

4 tbs of apple vinegar

3 tbs of dried parsley

2 tbs of dried marjoram

¼ tsp of ground red pepper

¼ tbs of mustard

For homemade apple purée:

5-6 medium sized apples

1 tsp of ground cinnamon

4 cups of water

METHOD:

1. First you want to make an apple purée several hours earlier and put in the refrigerator.

2. For homemade apple purée; start by washing and peeling the apples, then cut into quarters and remove the core. Place them into a large pot and pour enough water to cover them (4 cups will do the job). Bring them to the boiling point and keep cooking until soft, stirring occasionally. After about 20 minutes, remove from the heat and drain. Allow them to cool for a while and mash with a fork. Place in a food processor with one tsp of ground cinnamon. Mix for 30 seconds, or until a smooth mixture. Pour in a tall jar and cover with a tight lid.

3. Now you want to prepare your starter. Whisk the coconut oil, apple vinegar, ground red pepper and mustard into a large bowl, until you have a smooth mixture. Combine with an apple puree and add dried parsley and dried marjoram. Let it stand in the refrigerator for about an hour. You can serve your healthy starter or you can combine with a salad.

MAINS

92

"Fish, to taste right, must swim three times —in water, in butter, and in wine."

~ POLISH PROVERB

GREEN CABBAGE SALAD

INGREDIENTS:

3 cups of organic green cabbage, chopped

2 small organic red onions, peeled and sliced

2 organic carrots, peeled and sliced

2 garlic cloves, crushed

2 tbs of coconut oil

1 cup of water

METHOD:

Use a large pot to heat up the coconut oil. Add the cabbage and stir well. Next add the carrots and onion slices. Reduce heat to a minimum and slowly add 1 cup of water. Cover and simmer for about 30 minutes. Stir occasionally. When all the water evaporates, add the garlic and remove from the heat. Serve warm.

LAMB CUTLETS & PEPPERS SALAD

INGREDIENTS:

3 thin grass fed lamb cutlets

2 organic green peppers, chopped

1 medium organic tomato

1 small organic onion

1 tbs of coconut oil

Rock/sea salt and black pepper to season

For the marinade:

¼ cup of apple vinegar

¼ cup of lemon juice

1 tsp of ground pepper

2 tbs of vegetable oil

METHOD:

1. Mix the marinade ingredients in a small bowl. Soak the lamb cutlets in the marinade and keep in the fridge for about an hour. Remove from the fridge and fry in a grill pan, on a medium temperature, for about 15 minutes on each side. You can add some water while frying (½ cup should be enough). Remove from the grill pan and cut into small cubes.

2. Wash and cut the tomato into thin slices. Peel and cut the onion. Mix with other ingredients, add cutlets and season with oil, salt and pepper.

MAINS

TASTY EGGS & ONIONS

INGREDIENTS:

4 boiled free range organic eggs

2 medium organic onions

1 grated organic carrot

1 cup of organic baby spinach, chopped

1 tbs of grated fresh ginger

1 tbs of lemon juice

1 tbs of coconut oil

1 tsp of ground turmeric

Rock or sea salt to season

METHOD:

Peel and cut the onions. Salt them and leave it to stand for 15-20 minutes. Rinse well and press gently to drain any excess liquid. Sprinkle some lemon juice over it and set aside. Meanwhile, boil the free range organic eggs for about 10 minutes, remove from the heat, peel and cut into small cubes. Combine it with the baby spinach, grated carrot and ginger. Add the onions and season with coconut oil, salt, and turmeric. Refrigerate for at least one hour before serving.

MAINS

ROAST VEGGIES WITH FETA GOAT'S CHEESE

INGREDIENTS:

200 gram pack of goats feta cheese

½ cup of beetroot, peeled and diced

½ cup of organic brussel sprouts, chopped

½ cup of pumpkin, peeled and chopped

½ cup of organic carrot, chopped

1 cup of spinach leaves, finely chopped

1 cup of fresh organic tomatoes, roughly chopped

½ cup of roasted tomatoes

1 small onion, sliced

2 garlic cloves, minced

Sea salt and black pepper to season

3 tbs of coconut oil

METHOD:

1. Preheat the oven to 350 C. In a large bowl, combine the goats feta cheese, beetroot, brussel sprouts and pumpkin. Add 1 tbs of coconut oil and a pinch of salt. Place on an oven tray and bake for about 20 minutes. Meanwhile, heat up the remaining oil in a medium sized saucepan. Add onions and carrot, and fry for about 5 minutes, stirring constantly.

2. Add the diced tomatoes and spinach. Season with pepper and gently simmer for about 20 minutes. Stir once and then add spinach, salt, and pepper. Serve warm.

MAINS

THAI AVOCADO WITH GINGER

INGREDIENTS:

1 cup of fresh avocado, chopped into cubes

3 tbs of ginger sauce

1 tbs of coconut oil

2 tbs of fresh ginger, ground

2 cloves of garlic

2 tbs of fresh chilli peppers, minced

½ cup of fresh button mushrooms

1 large organic red bell pepper, sliced

2 tbs of teriyaki sauce

¼ cup of water

¼ cup of fresh basil, chopped

1 small onion, peeled and sliced

METHOD:

1. Combine the ingredients in a non-stick frying pan or a wok. Heat up the stove to a medium temperature and fry the ingredients for about 20 minutes, stirring constantly.

2. Serve with chicken or a meat of your choice.

PUMPKIN DELIGHT

INGREDIENTS:

2 cups of chopped pumpkin

2 tsp of fresh cumin

2 tsp of ground coriander

4 tbs of coconut oil

8 dried figs, sliced

1 red onion, sliced

¼ cup of fresh coriander, chopped

4 tbs of fresh lemon juice

¼ cup of coconut oil

METHOD:

1. Preheat the oven to 300 C.

2. In a large bowl, combine the pumpkin with cumin, coriander, and coconut oil. Mix well. Spread this pumpkin mixture on a baking sheet and bake for about 20 minutes. Remove from the oven and allow it to cool.

3. Place cooked pumpkin, into a bowel with figs, onion, coriander leaves, lemon rind, lemon juice and add more coconut oil, toss gently to coat. Serve.

SWEET POTATO WITH ONIONS

INGREDIENTS:

3 medium organic sweet potatoes

1 large organic onion, peeled and sliced

2 tsp of coconut oil

½ tsp of salt

1 tbs of parsley, chopped

METHOD:

1. Peel and cut the potato into thin slices. Add to boiling water and cook until tender. Remove from the heat, drain and allow it to cool.

2. Peel and cut the onion into small pieces. Add to boiling water and cook until tender. Rinse well under cold water and squeeze gently. Combine with potato slices and season with the salt and chopped parsley. Top with melted coconut oil.

MAINS

SUPER SAUSAGE SALAD

INGREDIENTS:

8 thick hormone free beef sausages
(gluten & wheat-free)

1 medium organic sweet
potato, boiled

1 organic red onion, peeled
and sliced

3 tbs of extra virgin coconut oil

Rock or sea salt and pepper
to season

1 tsp of apple vinegar

METHOD:

Heat up the coconut oil in a
large frying pan over a high
temperature. Fry sausages for
about 30-40 minutes. Remove from
the pan and allow it to cool for
about 30 minutes. Cut into slices
and combine with sweet potato
and red onion slices. Season with
salt, pepper and vinegar. Let it
stand in the refrigerator for 30
minutes before serving.

BARBECUED SALMON WITH ASPARAGUS

INGREDIENTS:

4 thick salmon fillets

1 cup of asparagus, chopped

1 tbs of basil, chopped

1 tbs coriander, chopped

2 tbs coconut oil

METHOD:

Heat up the coconut oil in a
saucepan over a medium-high
temperature. Fry salmon fillets
for about 5 minutes on each
side. Remove from the saucepan.
Add chopped asparagus to the
same saucepan. Reduce the heat
to medium and fry for about 5
minutes, stirring occasionally.
Now return the salmon fillets to
the pan, heating slowing, stir well.
Serve warm.

MAINS

"The main facts in human life are five:
birth, food, sleep, love and death."

- E.M. FORSTER

BRITISH CHIA SEEDS

INGREDIENTS:

2 cups of chia seeds

2 tbs of tomato sauce

1 tsp m alt vinegar

2 tsp of salt

2 cups of water

METHOD:

1. It is best to soak the seeds for 8-12 hours, but if you can't ,then cook them in water for 35 - 45 minutes until they start to soften.

2. When chia seeds start to soften, add other ingredients. Cook until seeds are soft enough that they will mash easily with a large spoon.

3. Make sure there is a small amount of liquid in the mixture until the very end of the cooking process. It is best to add half a cup of water at a time, stirring frequently.

SPICED FREE RANGE ORGANIC EGGS

INGREDIENTS:

4 free range organic eggs, beaten

1 small organic onion, chopped

1 small chilli pepper, chopped

1 tbs of almond butter (no sugar)

¼ cup of coconut milk

1 small tomato, chopped

1 tsp of dry coriander leaves

METHOD:

Melt the almond butter over a medium heat. Add the onion and chilli, frying for about 5 minutes, or until the vegetables soften. Now add the tomato, stirring and frying until the water evaporates. Meanwhile, combine the free range organic eggs with coconut milk and dry coriander leaves. Pour this mixture into the frying pan and fry for another 2-3 minutes.

MAINS

SWEET POTATOES & SAUSAGE SUPPER

INGREDIENTS:

1 hormone-free organic chicken sausage

2 organic sweet potatoes

3 free range organic eggs

¼ cup of coconut milk

1 tsp of coconut oil

METHOD:

1. Preheat the oven to 350 C. Wash and peel the sweet potatoes. Cut each potato in half and bake on tray in oven for about 50 minutes. Remove from the oven and let it stand for about 10 minutes. Now scoop out the middle of each potato and set aside.

2. Melt the coconut oil in a frying pan. Fry the chicken sausage for a few minutes and remove from the frying pan. Chop into small pieces.

3. In a separate bowl, whisk free range organic eggs and coconut milk. Add scooped parts of sweet potatoes and mix well. Combine this mixture with the chopped chicken sausage and fill each potato half with it. Put it back in the oven and bake for few more minutes until ready to serve.

CHICKEN KEBAB

INGREDIENTS:

2 hormone-free organic chicken breasts, boneless and skinless, cut into cubes

2 small organic sweet potatoes, peeled and cut into thin slices

1 medium organic red onion, sliced

1 organic red pepper, sliced

2 small organic tomatoes, sliced

3 tbs each of chopped parsley, mint and chives

6 tbs of coconut oil

For the marinade:

2 tbs of lemon juice

2 green chillies, seeded and finely chopped

2 small garlic cloves, finely chopped

4 tbs of coconut oil

2 tbs white wine vinegar

METHOD:

Boil the potatoes for about 20 minutes, until soft. Drain and allow it to cool. In a large bowl mix the lemon juice, green chilies, chopped garlic cloves, coconut oil, and vinegar. Soak the meat and the vegetables in this marinade and let it stand in the refrigerator for at least one hour.

Arrange the meat and vegetables on wooden sticks. Use a kitchen brush to spread the remaining coconut oil over the chicken kebabs. Barbecue directly over a medium temperature for about 5-6 minutes on each side.

"You don't have to cook fancy or complicated masterpieces — just good food from fresh ingredients."

~ JULIA CHILD

SPICY ORGANIC LAMB KOFTA KEBABS

(By Jessica Le Gray)

INGREDIENTS:

1 lb of organic lamb, minced

1 small organic onion, diced

1 free range organic egg

1 sweet organic bell pepper, chopped

3 cloves of garlic crushed or diced finely

1 chilli pepper

1 tbs turmeric

1 tbs paprika

1 tsp cayenne pepper

Pinch of rock or sea salt and black pepper

METHOD:

1. Combine all Kebab ingredients together in a bowl until evenly spread. Make into sausage-meat-like consistency and shape into long Kebab shapes. (Top tip; eliminate all the air gaps so the kebabs do not fall apart). Fry in 1 Tbs coconut oil for about 30 mixtures until brown.

2. Serve with fresh salad of sliced organic tomatoes, cucumbers and peppers, herb salad of fresh parsley, coriander and spinach. To make the garlic mayonnaise simply mix half a cup mayonnaise with 2-3 garlic cloves (crushed) to taste. For the chilli sauce, mix organic tomato puree, with finely diced onion, finely chopped coriander and chillies to taste.

MAINS

Did you ever stop to taste a carrot? Not just eat it, but taste it? You can't taste the beauty and energy of the earth in a Twinkie."

~ ASTRID ALAUDA

GRILLED LAMB & VEGETABLES

INGREDIENTS:

1 lb of hormone free, organic lamb meat, boneless and sliced

1 medium organic yellow pepper, chopped

1 medium eggplant/aubergine, peeled and sliced

1 organic cucumber, peeled and sliced

2 tbs of coconut oil

½ tsp of ground cumin

1 clove of garlic, ground

2 tbs of fresh parsley, chopped

½ tsp of sea salt

¼ tsp of black pepper

METHOD:

1. Preheat the oven to 350 C. Heat up the coconut oil in a large saucepan over a high temperature. Slice the eggplant/aubergine lengthwise and fry for few minutes. Reduce the heat and add other vegetables. Season with salt, pepper, and cumin. Cover the saucepan and cook for about 15 minutes, stirring occasionally.

2. In a medium sized baking pan, spread the vegetables to make an even layer. Put the lamb meat on top and bake for 30 minutes.

CHILLI SALMON

INGREDIENTS:

4 thick slices of salmon fillets, cut into medium cubes

4 tbs of chilli sauce

2 tbs of fresh lime juice

3 tbs of coconut oil

METHOD:

Combine the sweet chilli sauce and lime juice in a bowl. Soak the salmon fillets into this mixture and allow it to stand for about 30 minutes. Heat up the coconut oil over a high temperature. Fry the fillets for about 8 minutes. Remove from the pan and use kitchen paper to soak the excess oil. Serve warm with vegetables of your choice like asparagus or cauliflower.

LEMON SHRIMPS

INGREDIENTS:

1 lb of large shrimps, peeled

2 tbs of lemon juice

2 fresh lemons, cut into thin slices

5 tbs of coconut oil

½ tsp of sea salt

½ tsp of red pepper, ground

½ tsp of black pepper, ground

1 tbs of garlic, minced

10 bay leaves

METHOD:

1. Wash and drain your shrimps. In a large bowl combine lemon juice, 3 tbs of coconut oil, sea salt, black and red pepper, bay leaves and garlic to make a marinade. Next soak the shrimps in the marinade. Cover the bowl and leave in the refrigerator for about 10 minutes.

2. Heat up 2 tbs of coconut oil at a high temperature in a grill saucepan. Fry shrimps for about 15 minutes, stirring constantly. If necessary, add some marinade while frying. Remove shrimps and place them on a plate. Use the marinade generously. Serve warm.

"The only time to eat diet food is while you're waiting for the steak to cook."

-JULIA CHILD

FILLET STEAK SALAD

INGREDIENTS:

1 thin hormone free, organic beef fillet steak

5 lettuce leaves

1 tsp of radicchio leaf chicory, chopped

2-3 arugula rocket leaves

4 tbs of coconut oil

3 lemon slices

1 organic tomato

¼ cup of ground walnuts

¼ tsp of salt

METHOD:

1. Wash and pat dry the steak. Season with rock salt and black pepper. Heat up the coconut oil over a medium temperature and fry the steak for about 10 minutes on each side, or until tender. Remove from the pan and soak the excess oil with kitchen paper. Cut it into cubes and set aside.

2. Wash and cut the vegetables and place in a large bowl. Add the meat and ground walnuts. Season with salt and decorate with lemon slices before serving.

MAINS

SEAFOOD SALAD - THE MEDITERRANEAN WAY

INGREDIENTS:

1 small pack of frozen mixed seafood

1 tbs of coconut oil

1 small onion, peeled

1 cup of organic cherry tomatoes, roughly chopped

1 tsp of dry rosemary, chopped

1 tbs of freshly squeezed lemon juice

¼ tsp of salt

METHOD:

1. Heat up the coconut oil in a saucepan. Fry the frozen seafood for about 15 minutes, over a medium temperature (Top tip; octopus takes the most time to become tender so it is best to start cooking this earlier than the other seafood). You can add some water if necessary – about ¼ of a cup will be enough. Stir occasionally. Remove from frying pan and allow it to cool for about an hour.

2. Meanwhile, chop the vegetables into very small pieces. In a large bowl, combine the vegetables with seafood and season with salt, rosemary, and lemon juice. Serve with wheat free and gluten free spaghetti or pasta.

Our lives are not in the lap of the gods, but in the lap of our cooks."

~ LIN YUTANG

"He was a bold man that
first ate an oyster."

- JONATHAN SWIFT

GRILLED SEA BREAM

INGREDIENTS:

1 fresh sea bream, scaled and gutted

1 bunch of fresh parsley, finely chopped

¼ cup of freshly squeezed lemon juice

4 tbs of coconut oil

¼ tsp of sea salt

METHOD:

Wash the fish thoroughly, and using your hands soak the fish in lemon juice and coconut oil. Grill it over a medium heat for about 15-20 minutes, until a nice golden brown colour. Remove from the heat and sprinkle with fresh parsley. Serve immediately.

FRIED TUNA STEAK

INGREDIENTS:

4 pieces of tuna steak (about 1 oz each)

½ tsp of organic red pepper

2 tbs of parsley, chopped

2 tbs of rosemary, chopped

6 tbs coconut oil

6 cloves of garlic, chopped

¼ cup of lemon juice

1 tsp of sea salt

METHOD:

1. In a large bowl, mix the lemon juice, 2 tbs of coconut oil, sea salt, red pepper, chopped parsley and chopped rosemary. Combine all the ingredients to get a smooth marinade. Place the tuna steaks in this marinade and cover with a tight lid. Let it stand in the refrigerator for about an hour.

2. Preheat 4 tbs of coconut oil over high heat. Fry tuna steaks for 5-6 minutes on each side. Remove from the saucepan and serve.

MAINS

123

GRILLED BEEF WITH ALMONDS

INGREDIENTS:

3 large hormone free, organic, beef steaks

1 large onion, cut into thin slices

4 cups of organic baby spinach, chopped

1 tsp of garlic, chopped

½ tsp of ginger, minced

¼ cup of lemon juice

¼ cup of almonds

1 tbs of lime juice

2 tbs of water

1 tbs of organic fish sauce, sugar-free

4 tbs of vegetable oil

METHOD:

1. Wash and pat dry the beef steaks. Cut into bite size pieces and set aside. Heat up the vegetable oil over medium heat and fry the onions until a golden brown colour. Add the chopped baby spinach and garlic. Mix well and fry for about 5 minutes, until the water from the spinach evaporates. Stir well and remove from the heat.

2. In a large bowl combine the baby spinach with ginger, lemon juice, water, almonds and fish sauce. Mix well with a fork. Soak the beef steak pieces in with your spinach and return to saucepan. Add some more water if necessary. Cook over a low temperature for about 30 minutes, stirring occasionally.

3. When the water evaporates, remove from the heat and add lime juice. Allow it to cool for about 20-30 minutes and serve.

MAINS

124

GREEN CHILLI CHICKEN

INGREDIENTS:

1 lb of organic, free range chicken breast

2 cups of organic spinach, chopped

1 cup of fresh orange juice

3 organic green peppers

3 chilli peppers

2 small organic onions, chopped

1 tbs of ground ginger

1 tsp of red pepper powder

4 tbs of coconut oil

Rock or sea salt to season

METHOD:

1. Wash and pat dry the chicken using kitchen paper. Chop into bite size pieces. Finely chop the onions and peppers and set aside.

2. Heat up the oil in a large frying pan. Add the onions and peppers and sauté for a few minutes. Now add the chicken breast pieces, ground ginger, red pepper powder, and salt. Stir-fry for ten minutes, or until the chicken turns light brown.

3. Meanwhile, combine fresh orange juice with spinach in a food processor. Mix well for 30 seconds. Add this mixture to the pan and fry until the spinach is well combined. Cover the pan, remove from the heat and let it stand for about 10 minutes before serving.

MAINS

FISH STEW

INGREDIENTS:

1 lbs of haddock or cod fillets

5 organic carrots

3 chilli peppers, sliced

3 medium organic tomatoes, roughly chopped

¼ tsp of pepper

¼ cup of celery roots, finely chopped

1 tbs of coconut oil

METHOD:

1. Peel the carrots and wash thoroughly in cold water. Cut into thin slices. Cook the carrots in a pot of boiling water for about 20 minutes, or until tender. Remove from the heat and drain. Set aside.

2. Heat up the coconut oil in a large pot. Add the carrots and fry for about 5 minutes, stirring constantly. Meanwhile, wash and cut the fish fillets into 1 inch thick chops. Add your fish fillets and 2 cups of water into a pot. Bring it to the boil and cover. Reduce the heat to minimum and cook for a further 30 minutes. Now add sliced chilli peppers, tomatoes, celery roots, and peppers. Fry the vegetables over a low temperature for about 8-10 minutes. Serve warm.

MAINS

PORK CHOP WITH PINEAPPLE

INGREDIENTS:

1.5 lbs of hormone free, organic pork chop, boneless

1 medium pineapple, peeled and chopped

3 tbs of coconut oil

½ cup of coconut milk

1 tsp of turmeric

¼ tsp of black pepper

METHOD:

1. Wash and dry the meat. Cut into bite size cubes. Combine the meat with 2 tbs of coconut oil, coconut milk, turmeric, pepper, and pineapple. Mix well and set aside for 15 minutes.

2. Use a large wok pan to heat up the remaining coconut oil. Remove the pork and pineapple from the marinade and fry for about 5 -7 minutes on each side. Next pour in the remaining marinade, cover the wok pan and cook for 30 minutes over a medium temperature. The marinade will become thick and the meat soft. Remove from the heat and serve.

MAINS

TURKEY DRUMSTICKS WITH CAROB

INGREDIENTS:

3 organic grass fed turkey legs

½ cup of almond milk

4 tsp of nutmeg, ground

3 tbs of carob, minced

3 12x16 inch aluminium foil

Red ground pepper

METHOD:

1. Preheat the oven to 350 C. Meanwhile, wash and clean the meat. Pat dry using kitchen paper. In a small bowl, combine the almond milk, nutmeg, and carob. Mix well and soak each turkey leg with this mixture. Sprinkle with red pepper to taste and wrap each turkey leg in aluminium foil.

2. Place the wrapped drumsticks on a baking sheet and cook for 40 minutes. Remove from the oven and allow to cool for a while before serving.

MAINS

MUSTARD CHICKEN

INGREDIENTS:

2 hormone free, organic chicken breast, boneless and skinless

¼ cup of apple vinegar

¼ cup of coconut oil

1 tbs of garlic, minced

2 tbs of mustard

¼ tsp of ground green pepper

1 tbs of coconut oil for frying

METHOD:

1. Wash and pat dry your meat. Place it on a cutting board and season with the ground green pepper. In a large bowl, combine the apple vinegar, coconut oil, garlic and mustard to make the marinade. Soak the chicken breasts into this marinade and make sure it is fully coated. Cover and place in the refrigerator for at least 2 hours. (Top Tip; the best option is to keep it in the refrigerator overnight).

2. You will need a large nonstick frying pan. Place it on medium heat and add 1 tbs of coconut oil. Put your chicken breasts in the pan and fry for 7-10 minutes on each side, until crispy and light brown in colour. Add some of the marinade mixture whilst frying the chicken. These juices will make the meat soft. Stir occasionally, and checking if the chicken is cooked through fully. Serve warm with salad or gluten free pasta.

MAINS

131

EGGPLANT/AUBERGINE & CHICKEN CASSEROLE

INGREDIENTS:

2 large organic eggplant/aubergines

1 cup of free range, organic chicken, minced

2 medium organic tomatoes

1 medium organic onion

1 tsp of coconut oil

Black pepper

1 tsp of parsley, chopped

METHOD:

Peel the eggplant/aubergines and cut lengthwise into thin sheets. Put them in a bowl, and leave them to sit for at least one hour. Roll them in beaten free range organic eggs. Fry in hot coconut oil. Cut the onion, fry and the add sliced peppers, tomato, and finely chopped parsley and add to your pan. Fry for a few minutes and then add the chicken. When the chicken is tender, remove from the heat, cool, add one egg and season with pepper. Put fried eggplant/aubergine and meat with vegetables in an ovenproof dish and make layers until you have used all the food. Bake for 30 minutes at 300 C.

MAINS

CHICKEN CUBES WITH LEEKS

INGREDIENTS:

1 lb of free range, organic chicken fillets, cut into cubes

2 cups of organic leeks, trimmed

3 tbs of coconut oil

Thyme leaves for decoration

Black pepper

METHOD:

1. Cut the leeks into small pieces and wash it under cold water, a day before cooking. Leave it overnight in a plastic bag.

2. Heat up the coconut oil in a large saucepan. Add chicken cubes and fry for about 15 minutes over a medium heat. Stir constantly until the meat is nice and soft. Reduce the temperature, add leeks, and mix well. Cook for 5-7 more minutes. When done, remove from the saucepan and pepper to taste. Decorate with few thyme leaves before serving.

MAINS

CHICKEN WINGS WITH TURMERIC SAUCE

INGREDIENTS:

4 pieces of free range, organic,chicken wings, skinless
1 cup of almond milk
1 tbs of coconut oil
2 tbs of almond flour
1 tsp of ground turmeric
¼ cup of coconut oil
½ tsp of dried rosemary
¼ tsp of red pepper
1 tbs of garlic, ground

METHOD:

1. Preheat the oven to 300 C. Combine the rosemary, red pepper, garlic and coconut oil in a large bowl. Place the chicken wings in the same bowl and let it stand in the marinade for about 30 minutes.

2. Meanwhile, melt coconut oil in a saucepan. Add the almond flour and stir for few minutes. Remove from the heat and stir in ground turmeric and almond milk. Return to the heat and cook for about 7-10 minutes, over a medium temperature.

3. Remove the chicken wings from the marinade and place on a baking sheet. Bake uncovered for about 20 minutes. Remove from the oven, pour the turmeric sauce over the meat and bake for a further five minutes. Serve with vegetables of your choice.

MAINS

135

VEAL STEAK WITH RED PEPPER SAUCE

INGREDIENTS:

1 lb of grass fed, hormone free veal steak, boneless 3 red organic bell peppers

1 small organic onion, peeled and chopped

1 tsp of dried rosemary

3 tbs of coconut oil

4 cloves of garlic, chopped

½ cup of water

Cooking coconut spray

METHOD:

1. Preheat oven to 350 C and lightly coat a baking sheet with cooking spray. Place the meat on a baking sheet and cook for 60 minutes.

2. Meanwhile, cut each pepper in half, removing the stem and seeds. Finely chop each pepper. Heat up the coconut oil in a saucepan and add the garlic and onion. Sauté until translucent. It should take no more than 5 minutes. Stir constantly. Add the peppers, rosemary and ½ cup of water (you can add some more water if the sauce is too thick). Bring it to the boil and reduce the heat to minimum. Cook for 10-15 minutes. Set aside.

3. When the meat is nice and tender, remove from the oven and transfer to a plate. Pour the pepper sauce over the meat chops and serve.

"*Red meat is not bad for you. Now, the hormone filled, antibiotic laden, blue-green meat—well, that's bad for you!*"

-- TOM SMOTHERS

SWEET POTATO STEW

INGREDIENTS:

2 cups of organic sweet potatoes, chopped into small pieces

4 small organic tomatoes, chopped

3 organic carrots, sliced lengthwise

1 medium organic onion, sliced

1 medium organic zucchini, chopped

1 cup of dried apricots

2 tbs of coconut oil

½ tsp of sea salt

2 cloves of garlic, ground

2 tbs of ginger, minced

1 tsp of cumin, ground

1 tsp of cinnamon, ground

¼ tsp of turmeric

½ cup of water

2 tbs of fresh lemon juice

METHOD:

1. Warm up the coconut oil over a medium temperature in a large saucepan. Add the onions and salt. Fry for about 5 minutes, stirring occasionally. Now add the carrots and fry for another 5 minutes.

2. Now add the spices and raise the heat. Stir well and add the tomatoes, zucchini and apricots. Pour in the water and bring it to a boil. Cover and reduce the heat. Simmer gently for about 20 minutes.

3. Next add the sweet potatoes and lemon juice. Cook uncovered until the potatoes they are soft and the water evaporates. Serve with cooked carrot.

MAINS

138

"If more of us valued food and cheer and song above hoarded gold, it would be a merrier world."

-J.R.R. TOLKIEN

BAKED MUSHROOMS IN TOMATO SAUCE

INGREDIENTS:

1 cup of organic button mushrooms

1 large organic tomato

3 tbs of coconut oil

2 cloves of garlic

1 tbs of fresh basil

Rock salt and black pepper to season

METHOD:

Preheat the oven to 300 degrees. Wash and peel the tomato. Cut it into small pieces. Chop garlic and mix with the tomato and fresh basil. Heat up the coconut oil in a saucepan and add the tomato in mixture. Add ¼ cup of water, mix well and cook for about 15 minutes, at a low temperature, until the water evaporates, stirring constantly. Wash and drain mushrooms. Place them in small baking dish and spread tomato sauce over it. Bake for about 10-15 minutes. Salt and pepper to taste.

TOMATO BACON FRITTATA

INGREDIENTS:

3 large slices of dry cure, hormone free bacon

1 cup of organic leek, roughly chopped

2 large organic tomatoes, chopped

1 cup of organic spinach, chopped

2 gelatine free range organic eggs

1 small avocado, sliced

¼ cup of fresh parsley, chopped

vegetable oil spray

½ tsp of salt

¼ tsp of pepper

METHOD:

1. Spray some oil over a medium saucepan. Heat it up over a medium temperature and add the bacon slices and leek. Fry for few minutes, until the leeks have softened. Now add the tomatoes and chopped spinach. Cook for a further 4-5 minutes, until all the liquid evaporates and the vegetables soften.

2. Meanwhile, beat 2 tbs of grass fed gelatine, 2 tbs of warm water and 4 tbs of hot water. Add salt and pour this mixture into the frying pan. Mix well with the vegetables and fry for about 3 minutes, stirring constantly.

3. Remove from the pan and serve with avocado slices. Sprinkle fresh parsley on top.

BEEF SIRLOIN WITH SLICES OF EGGPLANT/AUBERGINE

INGREDIENTS:

1 thin grass fed, hormone free
  beef sirloin

1 medium organic eggplant/
  aubergine

1 tsp of coconut oil

Chopped basil

Black pepper

METHOD:

Wash and pepper the meat. Grill
it on a barbecue pan for about
10 minutes on each side. Remove
from the pan. Peel the Eggplant/
Aubergine and cut into two thick
slices. Fry for a few minutes in the
same barbecue pan. Remove from
the heat and serve with the beef.
Sprinkle with chopped basil.

TURKEY FILLET WITH WALNUTS

INGREDIENTS:

3 grass fed organic turkey fillets
½ cup of walnuts
¼ cup of water
1 tbs of coconut milk
½ cup of cranberries
Rock or sea salt to season

METHOD:

Fry the fillets in a frying pan, over a low temperature, for about 15 minutes, or until tender. Remove the pan from the heat and add the coconut milk, cranberries and walnuts. Mix well and fry for a further 5-6 minutes, until the coconut milk evaporates, stirring constantly. Allow it to cool before serving.

"Salt is born of the purest of parents: the sun and the sea."

~ PYTHAGORAS

MAINS

GLUTEN-FREE BEEF BURGERS

INGREDIENTS:

2 pounds of grass fed, hormone & wheat free beef, ground

3 free range organic eggs

2 medium organic onions, peeled and sliced

2 tsp of coconut oil

½ cup of fresh tomato sauce

1 tsp of red pepper, minced

½ tsp of ground black pepper

METHOD:

1. Preheat the oven to 300 C.

2. Meanwhile, melt 2 tsp of coconut oil over a medium temperature in a nonstick frying pan. Add the onion slices and fry until translucent, stirring constantly. Remove from the frying pan and set aside. Allow the onions to cool before combining with the meat. In a large bowl, combine the meat with all other ingredients. Mix well to evenly distribute them. Divide the mixture into 5 pieces and shape the burgers.

3. Bake for about 30 minutes, or until the meat is done. Remove from the oven and serve with lettuce, and tomato in a wheat free and gluten free bun, or with some vegetables of your choice.

TURKEY AVOCADO SANDWICH

INGREDIENTS:

½ lb of free range, organic turkey fillets

2 thick slices of avocado

½ cup of organic button mushrooms, fresh

4 leaves of organic lettuce, washed

3 tbs of coconut oil

METHOD:

1. Cut the turkey breast fillets into half inch strips. Heat up the coconut oil in a large saucepan over a medium temperature. Cook the turkey strips, covered, for about 15 minutes.

2. Remove the turkey fillets from the saucepan and use kitchen paper to remove the excess oil. Transfer to a plate.

3. Pour the coconut oil from the saucepan and put the pan back on the heat. Slice the button mushrooms in half and add to the saucepan. Cook for about 3-4 minutes, over a medium heat, until all the water evaporates. Remove from the saucepan and allow it to cool for a while. Use avocado slices to prepare a tasty wheat and gluten free sandwich. Serve cold.

MAINS

SWEET BRUSSEL SPROUTS WITH BACON

INGREDIENTS:

3 rashers of hormone free, dry cured smoked bacon

1 lb of organic brussel sprouts

5 medium organic sweet potatoes

2 organic red onions, peeled and sliced

¼ cup of lime juice

1 tbs of fresh parsley

¼ tsp of red pepper

3 tbs of coconut oil

¼ cup of walnuts

METHOD:

1. Preheat oven to 300 C.

2. Add 3 tbs of coconut oil in a large frying pan. Heat up over a medium temperature and add in the bacon and onion slices. Cook until onions are translucent for approximately 4-5 minutes. Meanwhile, peel and cut potatoes into bite size cubes and cut the brussel sprouts in quarters. Add the potatoes and brussel sprouts into a frying pan and reduce the heat to minimum. Stir well until nicely coated and simmer for about 10-15 minutes. Remove from the heat. Season with red pepper and parsley. Sprinkle with fresh lime juice before serving.

MAINS

SMOOTHIES & JUICES

"It's difficult to think anything but pleasant thoughts while eating a homegrown tomato."

-LEWIS GRIZZARD

STRAWBERRY & ALMOND SMOOTHIE PUDDING

INGREDIENTS:

2 cups of fresh organic strawberries, chopped

¼ cup of almonds, ground

1 tbs of chia seeds, minced

1 cup of coconut milk

1 tbs of sugar free vanilla extract

METHOD:

Combine the ingredients in a blender and mix for about 30 seconds, starting on low a speed and increasing to high until the mixture is smooth. Pour this mixture into pudding glasses and refrigerate overnight until the chia seeds thicken. Serve cold. You can keep it in the refrigerator for approximately 2-3 days.

AVOCADO, BLUEBERRY & SPINACH SMOOTHIE PUDDING

INGREDIENTS:

1 cup of fresh organic blueberries

½ cup of organic baby spinach, chopped

1 cup of avocado, chopped

2 tbs of almonds, minced

1 cup of coconut milk

½ cup of ice cubes (optional)

METHOD:

Wash and drain the baby spinach. Combine spinach with other ingredients in a blender and mix for about 30 seconds until smooth. Serve cold.

SMOOTHIES & JUICES

153

BLUEBERRY & CARROT SMOOTHIE

INGREDIENTS:

1 cup of frozen organic blueberries

1 cup of coconut milk

1 cup of water

½ cup of organic carrots, grated

1 tbs of cornstarch

METHOD:

Combine the ingredients in a blender and mix for 30-40 seconds. Allow it to stand for a while and serve.

SMOOTHIES & JUICES

FULL FRUIT YOGHURT SMOOTHIE

INGREDIENTS:

1 small organic apple

1 small organic orange

½ glass of water

1 tbs of shredded coconut

1 tbs of minced chia seeds

2 tbs of coconut yoghurt

½ cup of ice cubes

METHOD:

Combine the ingredients in a blender for 30-40 seconds until smooth. Drink cold.

SMOOTHIES & JUICES

155

APRICOT CHAI SMOOTHIE

INGREDIENTS:

1 glass of coconut milk

1 tsp of sugar free vanilla extract

1 tbs of dried apricots, minced

1 tbs of chia seeds

1 tbs of coconut cream

Cinnamon

METHOD:

Mix well the ingredients in a blender for 30 seconds until fully combined. Serve cold.

SMOOTHIES & JUICES

At home I serve the kind of food I know the story behind."

~ MICHAEL POLLAN

COCONUT FRUIT SMOOTHIE

INGREDIENTS:

½ cup of organic blueberries

¼ cup of organic strawberries

½ glass of coconut milk

1 tbs of coconut yoghurt

1 tbs of cornstarch

1 tbs of sugar free vanilla extract

Cinnamon to season

METHOD:

Beat the coconut yoghurt and coconut milk with a fork. It will take about 5 minutes to get a nice, smooth mousse. Pour this mousse into a blender, add blueberries and strawberries, cornstarch and then mix for 20 seconds. Add some cinnamon and vanilla extract before serving.

"One cannot think well, love well, sleep well, if one has not dined well."

– VIRGINIA WOOLF

SMOOTHIES & JUICES

157

COCONUT & SWEET POTATO SMOOTHIE

INGREDIENTS:

1 cup of organic sweet potato puree

½ cup of coconut yogurt

1 tsp of sugar free vanilla extract

¼ tsp of cinnamon

1 tbs of coconut butter, softened

1 tbs of cornstarch

METHOD:

Mix the ingredients in a blender for a few minutes. Leave in refrigerator overnight. Serve cold.

SMOOTHIES & JUICES

Tell me what you eat, and I will tell you what you are."

~ ANTHELME BRILLAT SAVARIN

CREAMY BANANA SMOOTHIE

INGREDIENTS

1 cup of coconut yogurt
¼ cup of coconut milk
1 tbs of coconut flakes
1 large organic banana
1 free range, organic egg
1 tbs of cornstarch

METHOD:

Make this smoothie by mixing the banana, coconut yogurt, coconut milk, coconut flakes, egg and cornstarch in a blender for 30-40 seconds. Leave it in the refrigerator for about an hour before serving cold.

WILD BERRY SMOOTHIE

INGREDIENTS:

½ cup of mixed organic wild berries, frozen

1 organic banana

1 cup of fresh pressed orange juice

½ cup of coconut milk

½ cup of ice cubes

½ tsp of cinnamon

METHOD:

Combine all the ingredients in a blender for few minutes until smooth. Allow it to cool in the refrigerator for about an hour before serving cold.

When eating fruit, remember who planted the tree

~ VIETNAMESE PROVERB

SMOOTHIES & JUICES

STRAWBERRY MILK SMOOTHIE

INGREDIENTS

1 cup of fresh organic
  strawberries

1 ½ cup of coconut milk

2 tbs of cornstarch

½ tsp of cinnamon

1 tbs of coconut cream

METHOD:

Put all the ingredients in
a blender and mix for 30
seconds. Pour the mixture
into pudding containers and
freeze until nearly firm.

*As for
butter versus
margarine, I
trust cows more
than chemists."*

~ JOAN GUSSOW

PUDDING

"Life is uncertain.
So eat dessert first."

-ERNESTINE ULMER

CHERRY PUDDING

INGREDIENTS:

½ cup of fresh organic cherries

½ cup of coconut yoghurt, frozen

¼ cup of coconut milk

1 tsp of cherry extract

1 tbs of cornstarch

1 tbs of whipped coconut dessert topping, sugar free

METHOD:

1. Put cherries, coconut milk and cornstarch in a blender for 30 seconds until you get a smooth mixture. Meanwhile, combine the cherry extract, frozen coconut yoghurt and whipped dessert topping in a small bowl.

2. Pour both mixtures into tall glasses so that the frozen yoghurt is on top. Leave in the refrigerator overnight.

PUDDING

COCONUT RICE PUDDING

INGREDIENTS:

½ cup of organic rice, uncooked

2 cups of coconut milk

¼ tsp of salt

½ cup of cranberries/red grapes

½ tbs of sugar free vanilla extract

Cinnamon stick

METHOD:

Use package instructions to cook the rice. In a medium sized saucepan bring the coconut milk to boil and add in the cooked rice, salt, vanilla extract, stirring well. Cook for about 20 minutes, or until you get a creamy mixture. Stir in the cranberries and remove from the heat. Allow it to cool in the refrigerator before serving.

"Vegetables are a must on a diet. I suggest carrot cake, zucchini bread and pumpkin pie."

- JIM DAVIS

PUDDING

QUICK ALMOND PUDDING

INGREDIENTS:

¾ cup of ground almonds

1 tsp of unwaxed, organic orange peel, grated

¼ cup of grated coconut

¾ cup of goji berries

1 cup of coconut milk

½ glass of water

1 tsp of sugar free vanilla extract

1 tbs of cornstarch

METHOD:

First you need to mix the grated orange peel with the cornstarch, vanilla extract, and coconut milk. Cook on a low temperature for 10-15 minutes. Allow it to cool. Meanwhile, mix the almonds, grated coconut, goji berries and water in a blender for few minutes. Add the now cooled orange peel and blend for another 1-2 minutes. Pour the mixture into pudding bowls. Let it stand in the refrigerator for few hours before serving.

SEEDS SMOOTHIE PUDDING

INGREDIENTS:

1 cup of organic strawberries

1 cup of coconut milk

¼ cup of pumpkin seeds

¼ cup of hazelnuts, ground

1 tbs of coconut butter

1 tbs of sugar free vanilla extract

2 tbs of cornstarch

METHOD:

Combine all of the ingredients in a blender for 30-40 seconds. Pour into tall glasses and let it stand in the refrigerator for about 30 minutes. Serve cold.

PUDDING

CHIA SEEDS WITH COCONUT YOGHURT PUDDING

INGREDIENTS:

1 cup of coconut yoghurt

3 tbs of chia seeds

1 tsp of ground almonds

1 tsp of cornstarch

METHOD:

For this easy recipe, combine the chia seeds with the coconut yoghurt, ground almonds and cornstarch into a bowl. Blend in an electric mixer to get a smooth mixture. Allow it to cool in the refrigerator for about 30-40 minutes before serving.

(Top Fact - chia seeds are very popular, and referred to as a 'Superfood', because of their nutritional values.)

PUDDING

COCAO MOCHA PUDDING

INGREDIENTS:

1 tbs of cocao powder (sugar-free)
½ cup of almond milk
1 cup of coconut milk
½ cup of coconut cream
1 tsp of instant mocha
1 cup of ice cubes

METHOD:

Mix all of the ingredients in a blender until thoroughly mixed together. Pour into tall glasses and serve cold.

COCONUT CAKE CUBES

INGREDIENTS:

1 cup of almond/rice flour
¼ cup of coconut flour
¼ cup of coconut flakes
¼ cup of fresh coconut, chopped
¼ cup of coconut milk
3 tbs of chia seeds, minced
1 cup of water

METHOD:

Soak the fresh coconut into water and let it stand for about an hour. Meanwhile, combine the almond or rice flour coconut flour and coconut flakes together and blend in the electric mixer. Now add the soaked coconut pieces and chia seeds mixing well for a few minutes. Pour the mixture into a small bowl and leave in the refrigerator overnight. Cut into bite size cubes before serving.

PUDDING

AVOCADO SMOOTHIE PUDDING

INGREDIENTS:

1 medium ripe avocado, peeled and pitted

1 ½ cups of coconut milk

1 tsp of vanilla extract

METHOD:

Mash the avocado using a food processor. Stir in the milk and vanilla extract, mixing well. Allow it to cool before serving.

Food for thought is no substitute for the real thing."

~ WALT KELLY

PUDDING

SUPER GREEN PUDDING

INGREDIENTS:

1 cup of organic broccoli, chopped

2 cups of fresh organic spinach

½ cup of coconut yoghurt

1 tsp of chia seeds, minced

Mint leaves

¼ cup of water

METHOD:

Wash all the vegetables and put all ingredients, yoghurt, seeds and mint into a blender. Mix well for about 30 seconds. Pour into pudding bowls and keep in the refrigerator for about 1 hour.

MELON SMOOTHIE PUDDING

INGREDIENTS:

2 slices of melon

¼ cup of fresh organic strawberries

¼ of organic banana

½ tsp of cinnamon

¼ cup of chopped walnuts

1 tsp of cornstarch

METHOD:

Put all the ingredients into a blender leaving the cinnamon to the side, mixing until a smooth consistency. Pour into glasses and sprinkle with cinnamon. Keep in the refrigerator and serve cold.

PUDDING

We are living in a world today where lemonade is made from artificial flavours and furniture polish is made from real lemons."

~ ALFRED E. NEWMAN

BANANA PUDDING

INGREDIENTS:

3 large organic bananas
2 cup of coconut milk
½ cup of water
1 tsp of sugar-free vanilla extract
1 tsp of cinnamon

METHOD:

In a medium sized saucepan bring the coconut milk to the boil. Meanwhile, peel and cut the banana into thin slices. Add the banana slices, vanilla extract and cinnamon to the saucepan of milk. You can add some water if necessary. Cook for about 10 minutes over a medium heat, stirring constantly. Remove from the heat and pour into pudding bowls. Allow it to cool before serving.

TROPICAL FRUIT SALAD

INGREDIENTS:

1 organic kiwi, sliced

1 mango, sliced

½ cup of pineapples, chopped

2 bananas, sliced

½ cup of organic strawberries, sliced

METHOD:

Mix everything together in a large bowl. Serve with a spoonful of cool coconut whip and you are all set!

"High-tech tomatoes. Mysterious milk. Super-squash. Are we supposed to eat this stuff? Or is it going to eat us?"

~ ANNITA MANNING

EGG SMOOTHIE PUDDING

INGREDIENTS:

3 free range organic eggs

1 cup of almond milk

½ cup of water

1 tbs of coconut yogurt

1 tsp of sugar-free vanilla extract

¼ tsp of cinnamon

METHOD:

Combine all the ingredients in the blender and mix until smooth. Allow it to cool in the refrigerator for about an hour before serving.

ICE CREAM FRUIT SALAD

INGREDIENTS:

2 cups of coconut milk

½ cup of mandarin oranges

½ cup of pineapple, crushed

1 cup of dried apricots, chopped

½ cup of pomegranates (optional)

½ organic banana, chopped

½ cup organic, sugar free cherry puree

1 container frozen coconut cool whip

METHOD:

Use a medium sized mixing bowl to combine the coconut milk and the cherry puree. Add your fruits then add in the coconut cool whip. In a 9x 13 pan, spread the whole mixture evenly. Using foil to cover the pan and freeze. Serve cold.

PUDDING

NUTTY PUDDING

INGREDIENTS:

1 tbs of almonds, grated

1 tbs of walnuts, grated

1 tbs of macadamia nuts, grated

1 cup of organic blackberries

2 medium organic bananas

3 cups of almond milk

2 free range egg whites

1 tbs of cornstarch

METHOD:

Simply combine all the ingredients into a blender, mixing well for 40 seconds. Allow to cool before serving.

It would be nice if the Food and Drug Administration stopped issuing warnings about toxic substances and just gave me the names of one or two things still safe to eat."

~ ROBERT FUOSS

PUDDING

CHERRY PUDDING BELLS

INGREDIENTS:

2 lbs of organic cherries, pitted

2 lbs pineapple, crushed

1 package grass fed gelatine

2 cups of water

1 cup of fresh pressed organic orange juice

1 cup of raisins

METHOD:

Bring the water to the boil, add the gelatine and stir until dissolved, make sure to stop before this turns in to "Jello". Add all remaining ingredients and pour into a 9 x 13 pan and chill. Serve with cool coconut whip.

PUDDING

For further support, guidance
and help please see

www.HealEndometriosisNaturally.com

Lightning Source UK Ltd.
Milton Keynes UK
UKOW07f0112101117
312466UK00001B/25/P

9 781530 979219